The ESSENTIALS OF AN HONOURABLE *Marriage*

Rev. Dawn Nation-Wilson

FriesenPress

Suite 300 - 990 Fort St
Victoria, BC, Canada, V8V 3K2
www.friesenpress.com

Copyright © 2015 by Rev. Dawn Nation-Wilson
First Edition — 2015

ISBN
978-1-4602-6037-1 (Hardcover)
978-1-4602-6038-8 (Paperback)
978-1-4602-6039-5 (eBook)

1. Family & Relationships, Marriage

Distributed to the trade by The Ingram Book Company

Table of Contents

ACKNOWLEDGEMENT

Love begins at home with Gurad Wilson, (Gerry), my husband and my children, Mark Blackwood, Andrew Blackwood, Tamaira Blackwood and Samantha Blackwood. Without my family I would be still seeking love outside of my home. A big thank you to my husband, Gerry who has listened to me as I ponder ideas aloud and for giving me daily encouragement and to whom I have been married for more than 12 years. If all husbands loved their wives as Gurad does, fewer women would be looking elsewhere for love. I feel secure in the warmth of my husband's and my children's love of which I am feeling very blessed and grateful.

I want to express my gratitude to God (my Heavenly Father), My mother, Ivy Nation, My Father Raphael Nation, my sisters Linette Nation, Doreen Williams, Merva Richards, also my friends Dr. Sylvia Kemp, Dr. Mary Johnson, Dr. Merle Grant, Bishop Larry Gunter, Bishop Jackie Gordon, Pastor Util Murray, Alcedo Cruz, Vinessa Ellis, Gillian Samuels, Bridget Ubachi, Aldeen Morgan, Henroy Morgan, Andrea Bowea, Trisha Shearman, Joyce Drain, Jenny Holloman, Edith Williams Evadne Blake, Gwen Bailey, and Yvonne Friesen who have encouraged me to write this book.

I also wish to thank the many couples who testified that through my counseling and prayer that they are experiencing successful marriages, learning to understand each other's love language and experiencing their positive relationships while growing together.

My fervent prayer is that your lives and your marriages will give a true reflection of the One from whom every family in heaven and on earth is named. Remember my sisters and brothers that God's grace is sufficient to keep and His power is perfect in our weakness.

May we all say with Paul, "By the grace of God, I am what I am, and His grace was not poured out on me in vain...but I labored more than them all – yet, not me, but the grace of God in me."

God Bless you all.

INTRODUCTION

I choose to write my thesis on "The Essentials of an Honourable Marriage," because I believe that if Christian couples would practice the essentials of an honourable marriage, there would be fewer divorces and more successful marriages. The essentials of an honourable marriage are: faithfulness, patience, forgiveness, service, respect, kindness, and celebration. If Christians would allow the Holy Spirit to lead and direct their lives, their marriages would be an example of Christ and the church.

As couples plan their weddings, they should learn more about marriage, and receive counselling for at least six months on how to deal with the changes that will occur after marriage. Husbands and wives will learn how to grow together with love and understanding, instead of growing apart and coming to despise each other. Proper counselling will help couples to experience the loving, peaceful, and joyful relationship that God intended for their marriage union. God ordained marriage and uses it to illustrate his relationship with His people (the church). There is perhaps no greater tragedy than the violation of these sacred vows.

What is love? Love is an action word. "For God so loved the world that He gave his only begotten Son that whosoever believeth on Him should not perish but have everlasting life." *(John 3:16)* Couples must be willing to give to each other in order to experience a successful marriage. When one spouse takes from the other and gives nothing or very little in return, it can be very discouraging because one spouse gets burnt out by giving, while the other is strengthened by receiving. When marriages are based on love and understanding instead of on emotions, they are more successful because emotions fluctuate. "Emotion is a psychic and physical reaction subjectively experienced as strong feelings and physiologically involving changes that prepare the body for immediate vigorous action. This feeling is the continuous background of one's awareness marked by pleasure, pain, attraction, disturbance, excitement and repulsion." (Worthington, Jr., 1998)

There is no problem, difficulty, or defeat that you cannot solve or overcome by faith, positive thinking, and prayer to God. The techniques are simple and workable, and God will help you always when you call and depend on Him. So believe in God by faith and you will live a successful marriage life.

I would like to extend my appreciation for the invaluable use of the works of some of the following authors of which I am fascinated: Dr. Henry Cloud & Dr. John Townsend, Kay Arthur, Norman Vincent Peale, and Benjamin Carson.

Truths from the Holy Bible must be practiced in order to fulfill God's requirements, and for one to receive His promises. Knowing Jesus as Lord and Saviour will guide wives and husbands in this life and lead them into the life to come. Christian counselling is biblically based, and when it is understood and practiced, it will strengthen one's faith in God, their character, and fortify their mind and body against the evil of this world. As a Christian counsellor, my desire is to be a disciple for the people of God.

Many people marry today with the expectation that their partner will meet all their needs for emotional support and nurturing, for stimulating social interchange, friendship, partnership in shared activities, sexual stimulation and satisfaction, and family belonging. The partners usually do not bring their expectations for marriage into question because they are engaged in blaming each other for their unhappiness.

Chapter One
WHAT IS MARRIAGE?

Marriage is a joyous celebration of love. It is the mystery of two becoming one, beginning a life together, and making a commitment. The structure of marriage includes both commitment and intimacy. Commitment is a certainty from the spiritual perspective, and is designed by God. "Have you not read that at the beginning the creator made them male and female…For this reason a man will leave his father and mother and be united to his wife…Therefore, what God has joined together, let not man separate." *(Mat. 19: 4-6)*

Spouses can build commitment by constantly telling their partners of their love, and can show commitment by never flirting with another person, spending time with each other, and by being faithful in all their actions. "Submit to one another out of reverence for Christ. Wives, submit to your husbands as to the Lord…In this same way, husbands ought to love their wives as their own bodies. He who loves his wife loves himself." *(Eph. 5:21-22, 28)* "Husbands, in the same way be considerate as you live with your wives, and treat them with respect as the weaker partner and as heirs with you of the gracious gift of life, so that nothing will hinder your prayers." *(1 Pet. 3:7)*

"Being fruitful and multiplying is the way the purposefulness of marriage is described in Genesis. A couple shares the depths of despair but also the heights of joy in service to each other. Empathy and support happens when talking about their experience in the actions of each other in response to the other in the shared work. Our shared experience and our discussion of individual experiences unite us." (Garland, 1986)

Chapter Two
GOD'S AND MAN'S IDEA
FOR MARRIAGE

God's and man's idea for marriage are very different, because God's plan was that a marriage should last for a life time and man's plan is to get divorced when he is dissatisfied with marriage. God created the family as an institution because he wanted spouses to experience positive and productive marriages as they communicate openly with each other without fear of retribution, share their ideas, their dreams with each other, and listen without condemnation.

People are married for many different reasons, some for love, as a way of escape, for lust, for money, etc., because they do not understand the true meaning of love and marriage. Couples who are experiencing hurt should know that in the midst of their situations, there is hope, and that hope is through the Lord Jesus Christ. Jesus is definitely the answer in every situation. Some people experience hurt because of a physical problem, a mental attitude, or a spiritual sin experienced before marriage. Their hurt may be very severe that it renders them hopeless, leaving them without a will to live.

"When marital conflict arises and intensifies, or less attraction is shown or common interests become no longer common, it takes as evidence that this particular match was an unfortunate mistake." (Garland, 2003) However, spouses can meet intimacy by communicating feelings, talking about values, hopes, fears and emotions. They show caring and use their time to regulate their intimacy through their activities. Marriages operate according to re-patterns of behaviour. Some relationship problems in marriages are because of finances, in-laws, child discipline, fighting about sex, and blaming each other for their unhappiness, which involves power struggles.

Spouses must listen empathetically to each other with their ears, eyes, and hearts. They must listen for meaning and understanding, observe behaviour, and tune into their senses, and feelings. Instead of projecting their own feelings, thoughts, motives and interpretation, they will deal with the reality of their spouses' feelings. They will focus on receiving deep communication from each other. "The greatest need of a human being is psychological survival, which is secondary to physical survival. They want to be appreciated, validated, affirmed, and have a desire to be understood. When you listen with empathy to your spouse, you will give him or her psychological air and can focus on influencing or problem solving after that vital need is met. This need for psychological air impacts communication in every area of life." (Covey, 1989)

The Bible is the greatest teaching tool with God's guidelines written through the inspiration of the Holy Spirit. The Lord God said, "It is not good for the man to be alone. I will make a helper suitable for him…For this reason a man will leave his father and mother and be united to his wife: and they will become one flesh. The man and his wife were both naked, and they felt no shame." *(Gen. 2:18-25)*

Chapter Three

DEMONSTRATING THE ESSENTIALS OF AN HONOURABLE MARRIAGE

This new adventure called marriage is a fantastic journey of change, but to experience an intimate marriage relationship is a matter of the heart. Within the heart, marriage is either made healthy or it slowly deteriorates. Solomon said, "For as a man thinketh in his heart, so is he."*(Prov. 23:7)* The decisions you make or do not make can be the difference between having a great, warm, loving marriage or a distant, cold marriage. Faithfulness, patience, forgiveness, service, respect, kindness, and celebration will contribute to an exciting, loving, and wonderful relationship. You can make choices that will foster your love for God and for your spouse individually or as a couple. Once you agree in your heart, the day-to-day behaviour will begin to follow and will strengthen your marriage. Couples can build their relationships one day at a time; each person is responsible to monitor his/her own marriage and measure his/her own progress. In my heart, I know that the following essentials will bring honour to your marriage when practiced.

1. Faithfulness – I will be faithful to my spouse at all times and in all circumstances.

2. Patience – I will not try to change things about my spouse that I do not like, but will modify my own behaviours that annoy my partner.

3. Forgiveness – When my spouse offends me, I will forgive the offenses in my heart before I am being asked.

4. Service – I will anticipate my spouse's spiritual, emotional, physical, and material needs and will do everything I can to meet them.

5. Respect – I will not act or speak in a way that demeans, ridicules, or embarrasses my spouse.

6. Kindness – I will be kind to my spouse, eliminating any trace of meanness from my behaviour and speech.

7. Celebration – I will appreciate my spouse's gifts and attributes and celebrate them personally and publicly.

When spouses fully understand the essentials of an hounourable marriage, they can direct or correct the course of their marriage, realize that they can make heartfelt choices, and adjust their will to act more Christ-like toward their spouse. As Christians, spouses should aim for the stars in their marriages because aiming at higher standards of behaviour opens them to improvement. Couples should understand that marriage is a reality and not a dream before they make this big decision about their lives. Spouses are encouraged to develop their character through experiencing the love of Christ.

"[The] human heart is the location of the mind, will, and emotions, and the place where people make powerful decisions. Couples can stay happy together for the rest of their lives if they understand that a more intimate marriage relationship is a matter of the heart." (*Cloud & Townsend, 1999*) "Can two walk together except they be agreed?" *(Amos 3:3)*

"The mind is one of God's greatest achievements of creation because this is where the details of human experiences are stored.

The will provides the fuel the human heart needs to carry out the instructions commanded and is incredibly capable of both great good and great unkindness.

Emotions (feelings) are the way that you experience life and make a connection with yourself, your environment, and with others. Feelings can be conflicting because you can experience two opposing feelings at the same time. For example, sadness and anger can be felt at the same time and sometimes a person is unable to differentiate between the two. Feelings can also happen at an incredible, almost overwhelming rate. Feelings do not last forever; they all leave at some point because they are not facts. Feelings flood the human heart and make so many of the experiences wonderful and satisfying or sad and unsatisfying events in your life. God Himself has feelings, because one cannot read the Scriptures without feeling God's love, fury, compassion, and patience. Like Himself, God has created us to have feelings and a heart that possesses a great mind, will, and emotions." *(Weiss, 2005)*

Spouses must show love to each other, listen carefully with understanding, and be encouraging and supportive. You can make a difference in your marriage spiritually and naturally if you consistently practice these essentials to experience an hounourable marriage.

Marriage is a system of verbal and non-verbal communication as well as action. For example, if a husband buys flowers to show his love to his wife, he gives her the flowers and she gives him a kiss. When a spouse acts one way it influences the other to act another way; there is a system. Some couples have a system whereby one spouse leaves the dirty clothes on the floor, and the other spouse complains, but picks them up. As a result of this system one spouse has reinforced the behaviour that it is acceptable for the other spouse to continue leaving the dirty clothes on the floor. He or she is rewarded for putting dirty clothes on the floor, because the spouse picked up the dirty clothes, washed, ironed, folded, put inside drawers, or hung them in the closet, but the only penalty the untidy spouse received was listening to a complaint before they are picked up and taken care of.

One spouse can change the above system by deciding not to reward the other spouse's negative behaviour by not complaining, picking up the dirty clothes, washing, ironing or putting them away. Soon there are piles of dirty clothes on the floor. There is now a need for clean clothing and pain begins for the irresponsible spouse. This pain now motivates the untidy spouse to change his or her undesirable behaviour. If the tidy spouse can be consistent in not picking up after the irresponsible spouse, a new system will evolve. Soon there will be two people who are congruent in their behaviour, which will cause the problem to be solved. If the couples try to be more like Jesus by hounouring their marriages, this will bring harmony and their heavenly Father will be pleased.

Chapter Four

FAITHFULNESS

Faithfulness is the cornerstone upon which an hounourable marriage can be built and will thrive. Without faithfulness, your marriage will suffer seasons of damage. The following are seven different types of faithfulness:

1. **Spiritual faithfulness** means putting God first with absolute loyalty. This means that you as an individual will develop and maintain the spiritual muscle of faithfulness through prayer, study, fellowship, and service. A spouse will express faithfulness to God individually by aspiring to know, love, and serve Him only in greater measure. Spiritual faithfulness also means that you agree to grow together in Christ. The Christian faith can unite people, but it can also divide them. Encourage the individual not to try to "play God," and maintain a humble attitude rather than a judgmental one. Encourage the development of personal spiritual maturity through reading and studying God's Word and through faithfully practicing a life of prayer. Commit your mate to the Lord and by faith, claim conversion. Prayer and trust in God are of great value. God has a wonderful way of working things out and allows your mate to see Jesus in your attitude and actions. Let your love overflow. Paul says: "Love is patient, love is kind…Love never fails." *(1 Cor. 13:4, 8)*

9

Try to demonstrate that "the love of God has been poured out in your hearts." *(Rom. 5:5)*

2. **Emotional faithfulness** means that your spouse is the person with whom you share your heart or emotional self. Your spouse should not be second to your parents, friends, co-workers, or to your children. Your spouse is the person you allow to see you at the core of your being.

3. **Sexual faithfulness** means your spouse is the only person with whom you are sexually active. Sexual faithfulness must be maintained as the top priority in your relationship. You express faithfulness to your spouse by preserving the sexual exclusiveness of your relationship.

Couples must eliminate pornography and masturbation completely from the marriage union. Avoiding pornography from all sources is very critical to sexual faithfulness. Sexual faithfulness also includes spouses not flirting or giving sexual energy to other people. Spouses maintain sexual faithfulness by avoiding even a hint of interaction or flirtation with another person. Couples who have made this agreement – and kept it – do not have the damage and pain in their marriage relationship that other couples may experience. If you are struggling with sexual faithfulness, you can get immediate help by praying and seeking Christian counselling.

Intimate love is the building block for the structure of marriage relationship and it is necessary for proper growth and is often very hard work. People cannot grow healthy on mistrust, irresponsibility, hurt, blame, and criticism but they will grow when they are being responsible, loved, encouraged, and trusted. In

Him, the whole building is joined together and rises to become a holy temple in the Lord. Couples must ask his or her spouse what pleases him or her, then, apply the golden rule. The golden rule is, "Do unto others as you would have them do unto you." *(Mat. 7:12)* When you view every wrong attitude and action as a serious offense against God, you will begin to understand the concept of being one flesh and living for God.

4. **Financial faithfulness** can help to provide a service of safety and teamwork that will keep your marriage strong. Couples argue most in marriages about sex and money. It takes a life plan to create sexual and financial faithfulness. Your financial plan includes budget, retirement, college funds, and creating the wealth you perceive God has given you permission to create. Your plan will also include a commitment to tithing. Being financially faithful to God is one way to be financially faithful to each other. Maturity in this area of faithfulness will add many blessings into your marital life.

5. **Parental faithfulness** is crucial to include in your marriage because it can make a great difference in your family during the years of your active parenting. As a parent, you can do your part in being a godly father or godly mother, but you cannot control your spouse's lack of responsibility or over-responsibility. It is in your power to be a team player. Remember, children need more than your involvement in their activities – they need to be able to sense your faithfulness to them, and ideally sense it from both parents. Discipline and discipleship when done consistently by both parents proves to be very successful.

6. **Relationship Faithfulness** in marriage is the greatest relationship next to your relationship with Jesus. Marriage relationship

needs more time, love, and commitment to remain stable and healthy. Your best friend should be your spouse, because this will help couples to maintain an hounourable marriage. This great friendship within your relationship will cause you to love each other even when you can see each other's weaknesses. You can laugh with each other about your mate's faults, be there when he is in pain, and are always available when she needs a little extra help. Spouses should learn that each person should only be responsible for his or her own relational faithfulness.

Marriage is built on faith in God. Everything we see existed in the invisible state before God made it visible. Therefore, faith is not geared to what does not exist – it relates to everything that is not seen. Faith is "being sure of what we hope for and certain of what we do not see." *(Heb. 11:1)* Faith deals with potential – what you *yet* can see, do, be and experience. Faith says, "I cannot see it, but I believe it is there. Faith never deals with what you have done, but with what you have yet to do." *(Munroe, 1991)* Spouses must ask God with faith for their marriage to be successful, because faith is what deals with unseen things.

Spouses must focus on faith in order to experience a successful marriage. When their faith is in focus, they will be able to accept constructive criticism, handle unjust blame with poise and appropriate emotional response. As a result, they will find themselves at ease and be able to enjoy and value close relationships. They can be honest and open about their feelings, and laugh about their mistakes as they attempt to learn and profit from them. They can also welcome new challenges which will enable them to give themselves and others credit when it is due. Having faith in focus is the meaning of biblical faith that is, trusting God so that they can make the most out of every situation. Remember that joyous faith is focused on the person and work of Jesus Christ. "Looking away to Jesus, who is the

Author and Finisher of our faith. He, for the joy that was set before Him, endured the cross, despising and ignoring the shame, and is now seated at the right hand of the throne of God." *(Heb. 12:2)* Spouses should pledge to be faithful to each other at all times and in all circumstances in the fear of the Lord Jesus Christ.

Chapter Five
PATIENCE

Patience is a fruit, and fruit takes time to mature. You will need the nutrients of God's Word, the water of His Holy Spirit, and the light of honesty in your heart as God exposes your impatience. James said, "My brethren, count it all joy when ye fall into divers temptations; knowing this, that the trying of your faith worketh patience. But let patience have her perfect work, that ye may be perfect and entire, wanting nothing." *(James 1:2-4)* Do not try to change things about your spouse that you do not like but modify those behaviours that annoy your partner.

Spouses are very disappointed when they enter marriage thinking that it should make them happy. It is not the responsibility of your spouse to make you happy. Each spouse must make a choice to make himself or herself happy, because to place this expectation on someone else is very unreasonable. Practicing the essentials of an hounourable marriage will take the focus off your attempts to change your spouse and place the focus on you, which will help you to become more like Christ.

The Holy Spirit is able to mold your character more and more into the character of Christ through the relationship you have with your spouse. The strengths and spiritual gifts that each spouse possesses are only a limited expression of God's nature, and is a small reflection of His completeness. Together you will become more like

Christ. As Christians, you should seek to possess the personality of Christ and not one of your own. Remember that although your spouse is imperfect, he or she is still the son or daughter of the Most High God. How you treat your spouse is dependent on your relationship with God. You can be a vineyard of patience for your lover, best friend, spouse, and child of God daily.

"Detachment allows you to take a step back and diffuse the situation. You may even need to step back and say aloud 'This is not about me,' because this is just who your spouse is. He or she is not trying to be mean or spiteful. If you can step back, you will be able to react more patiently to the behaviour of your spouse. The way you think personally about your spouse's behaviour will dictate how you will respond to him or her. If you see the behaviour as a personal attack, believing your spouse is 'out to get you,' your response will most likely be less patient and more defensive. If you can see your spouse just being himself or herself, you may be able to detach enough to be patient. You can control how you see your spouse's behaviour either as a blessing of having an imperfect and human spouse who loves you or as an all-out alien attacking you, to steal the joy out of your life. You can choose to refuse your previous interpretation of your partner's annoying behaviour as deliberate offences or choose a more gentle and patient way to respond.

"After you apply prayer and detachment, use your patience to stop believing, that your spouse's behaviour is deliberate, and remember that God has only called you to love your spouse. You are limited to the power of changing yourself, and powerless to change any human being, including your spouse, because only God can change a person. You will be less angry and more patient, and will realize that you cannot change your spouse, because God has already made this impossible to do so."(*Weiss, 2005*).

Spouses can experience the power of patience, which is an intentional force that will increase their patience toward each other. The

Bible says, "He that is slow to anger is better than the mighty; and he that ruleth his spirit than he that taketh a city." *(Prov. 16:32)* Your impatience is the food source of anger, because as you react or over-react, the anger becomes stronger. When there is a disagreement between you and your spouse and you become impatient, your impatience will turn the focus toward your spouse, and make the situation impossible to deal with. You cannot use a faulty rationale to try to change the circumstances. As you exercise patience, you will be confident and calm in the way you respond to your spouse. With patience, your spouse will soon be willing to open up about the situation. It is always better to have the experience of responding patiently rather than impatiently.

Patience is a seed. "When you perform an act of patience such as a listening ear, silence about a spouse's mistake, or a laugh instead of a glare, you are sowing patience into your spouse's being. Patience allows you to discipline your responses positively to the difficult behaviour you are dealing with from your spouse. Your patient response will become a powerful seed that takes time to mature.

Sometimes you will sin in your behaviour toward your spouse and will need his or her patience. Keep planting the seed of patience in the soil of your spouse's life. There will be days when you will reap the fruit of patience that has been grown. Remember that the sin nature will remain inside you until death and at some time in your life, you will need your spouse to sow patience into your spirit.

Chapter Six

COUNSELLING AN UNHAPPY COUPLE

I have never met a couple that married with the intension of making each other miserable. Most people want to have a loving, supportive, and understanding spouse. I am convinced that the fastest way to have a loving spouse is to become a loving, supportive, and understanding spouse.

The Assessment Summary presented is about an unhappy wife, and a husband who is unaware of their difficulties. "John Brown (thirty-three) and Mary Brown (thirty-one) were both saved as adults and have sought counselling in order to improve a marriage relationship that is in trouble. The difficulty seems to be mostly a relationship problem. John and Mary seem to be functioning well, in spite of the employment pressures to which each is exposed. Both have good self-esteem and are not subject to experiencing psychological problems or mood disturbance." (Worthington, 1998)

As Everett Jr. Worthington states, "Seeing couples together, setting time limits, doing assessment, intervention, and termination is crucial to helping couples benefit from counselling. The couple should share setting goals, which should be positive and realistic. Goals should be derived from the Assessment and be specific in predictable areas. Throughout the counselling the counsellor will use ultimate goals, mediating goals, and working goals." (1998) In working together using such practical methods, couples will be given strategies to see tangible improvements in their union that are mutually rewarding. Envisioning a healthy marriage while practicing these recommendations will allow couples to be both investors and beneficiaries of marital success.

Relationship History

John and Mary have known each other for a little over six years. They met, dated for eight months and were engaged for twelve months – a period that they described as being one of their best periods, though they fought sometimes during it.

They have been married for two years. Their honeymoon was enjoyable though they had a large fight on the first day back from their honeymoon. Their lives together after taking their vows were characterized by hard work that was intense and draining. As a result, they became very tired at nights and their different days off allowed less time together.

In the month of June, they noticed that their relationship was changing in ways that were not pleasing. Two things happened at that time that affected their intimacy. First, they bought a house, and then Mary's friend came to live with them. Some of her friend's habits increased the tension in the household, forcing them to adjust to the presence of a third person and interfering with the intimacy patterns that they have established. After Mary's friend moved out, a future sister-in-law moved in.

Nature of Presenting Complaints

John and Mary share the view that their relationship could be improved, although they have different views of the nature and the severity of the problems within the relationship. In itself, this difference in perception indicates that attention needs to be paid to improving the relationship.

John views the disturbance as relatively mild. He feels that communication could be improved, that he could control his temper better during disagreements, be a better listener, and be more understanding when Mary has a rough day at the office. He also feels that they could argue less and show more outward signs of their love for each other.

Mary views the marriage as one in serious trouble. She complains of frequent arguments that are sometimes loud and long and of being afraid to argue with John at times because of his strong reactions. She also complains of an emotional pulling back, where physical presence or emotional closeness is no longer experienced. She added that John is not listening to her, not taking what she says seriously, or even showing enough affection (not just sexual contact) or doing enough things together.

Mary reacts to this by expressing her dissatisfaction with John. Though she tries to present suggestions in a positive way, it sometimes comes across as accusatory, which places John on the defensive. My perception of John's behaviour is that when he gets defensive, he jokes and makes light of the situation to try to diffuse the threat to argue. If that fails, a heated argument often ensues. John's defensiveness and Mary's (sometimes) accusatory style perpetuate the cycle of arguing. John's joking merely strengthens Mary's belief that he does not take her complaints seriously.

Concerning the seriousness of the relationship disturbance, I am inclined to agree with Mary's perception that the relationship has some disturbances that need considerable attention. If for no other reason, she believes the relationship to be in some trouble. I do not believe that John is the primary cause of the trouble. I attribute the cause of the trouble to some habits that *both* have in their relationship with each other – habits that can be changed if both are willing to work on changing. There is definitely some room for improvement in the marriage.

Relationship Strengths

This relationship has numerous strengths and has the potential to be a permanent one for the couple. Their strengths are:

- Love and respect for each other, support for each other, and enjoyment of being with each other. They are visibly proud of being together and are very supportive of each other.

- They are committed to sticking with the relationship and working problems out, rather than to pursue divorce. Both John and Mary seem to enjoy each other's company. They have more common interests than the average couple.

- They now actively seek to please each other, and have a good knowledge of what makes them happy. They often seek to provide those things for each other. An important strength in their marriage is that they enjoy a mutually pleasing sexual relationship.

- They have family members of origin in town who are supportive. (Paradoxically this can also be problematic if they depend on family members during marital disagreements, rather than personally working out their difficulties).

- John and Mary's strength is demonstrated on the Couple's Pre-Counselling Inventory, except for a few areas.

John and Mary gave evidence that they shared the same values and perceptions of their lives together. This relationship is built on a relatively solid foundation.

Relationship Weakness

There are three weaknesses in the marriage that seem to be the root of the problem: intimacy, communication, and conflict-resolution style. It is evident that these three areas would solidify a relationship that largely has a lot going for it. Failure to attend to these differences could be disastrous for the relationship and for each individual's self-esteem.

Intimacy – Five areas of intimacy were assessed. One general observation from the inventory is the marked differences in John's and Mary's perceptions of the current relationship. In general, John seems to report that the relationship is going well, just as he would like, and few changes are necessary. On the other hand, Mary sees the relationship as being in some serious difficulty and does not feel that she is getting her needs met. This is especially true of emotional intimacy. The inventory results fit with their general style of behaviour during counselling sessions and with their complaints.

Most of the information about intimacy is derived from the PAIR Inventory. According to authors Mark T. Schaefer and David H. Olson, the PAIR Inventory is "a 36-item measure of relationship intimacy, encompassing five different factors and one 'faking' [or imagined] scale. The five factors include:

"(1) Emotional Intimacy – feeling closeness, the ability to share feelings and be supported without defensiveness. (2) Social Intimacy – having common friends and a social network. (3) Sexual Intimacy – sharing affection, touching, physical, and sexual closeness. (4) Intellectual Intimacy – sharing ideas and experiences about life and work. (5) Recreational Intimacy – sharing of experiences, common pastimes, and involvement in activities. (1981)."

It should be noted that the scale can either be expressed in terms of how the relationship is now or it can be expressed in terms of how the relationship should be (or both), depending on what the researcher wishes to study. Respondents answer each item on a 5-point scale ranging from 1 (strongly disagree) to 5 (strongly agree). (Schaefer, M. T. & Olson, D. H., 1981). As for Mary and John, it would seem that the large differences in their perceptions are a great cause for concern.

Communication – Observations of the couple during assessment sessions and the responses on the PAIR Inventory indicate that there are some problems with the communication styles that are detrimental to the relationship. Both people are contributing to this problem, therefore, both people need to change their communication patterns, if the marriage is going to continue and improve.

A repeatable pattern of communication involves Mary, while sincerely desiring to help John. She criticizes about his behaviour or complains about something. Generally, John responds by laughing to try to keep the atmosphere light. Mary interprets this as John refusing to take her complaints seriously. She escalates the complaints or criticisms. This ultimately provokes John to respond in an effort to defend himself. As the criticism-defense cycle continues, John escalates his responses, becoming louder, and so does Mary. The emotional intensity of the arguments threatens and frightens Mary, who becomes reluctant to engage in future discussions with John for fear that she will provoke a fight. Therefore, she tries to get John to change by making helpful suggestions (criticisms), which continues the cycle.

Before the problem-solving discussion that was videotaped, John and Mary's moods were fairly cooperative and congenial.

Afterwards, they vented negative feelings and periodic unpleasant words were exchanged. This was of some concern to me, because it indicated that disagreements that were not resolved could eventually poison the interactions that occur following an agreement.

Another area of communication that needs attention includes sexual communication. The Browns need to communicate their sexual desires clearly and unambiguously to enable each party to read each other's signals. This is most obvious from the couple's Pre-counselling Inventory. When asked about how many times during the past month they had initiated sexual contact, John said six times but Mary only recognized one advance. Mary said that she had initiated sexual interaction six times but John only recognized one advance.

Problem Solving – Based on the videotaped discussion, an area of disagreement was the instruction about the resolution of the issue. First, the problem was never clearly defined and they jumped from one topic to another. Second, most of the time was spent in cross-complaining; there was no attempt to specify exactly what the problem was or to arrive at a solution. The problem was discussed mostly in the past (about who caused the problem) or was localized within the personality of one person. (Mary defined the problem as something wrong with John.) Positive comments about each other that occurred during the conversation were generally vague. Negative comments were very clear. The result is that the couple is better able to discern what is wrong than what is right with them.

Recommended Treatment Goals

Intimacy

1. Increase the emotional intimacy. John needs to listen carefully to Mary in order to identify and acknowledge her feelings. Mary needs to offer positive support for John and not criticism.

2. Increase the frequency of sexual contact, given that the quality of the contact is good when it occurs.

3. Set aside a regular time that the couple can be together and talk about intimate things.

Communication

1. Increase positive interactions.

2. Use the videotape to improve communication styles.

3. Spend more time in each other's presence.

Problem Solving

1. Use videotaped practice to learn to communicate problem solving in ways that will get to some resolution of disagreements and will not carry over into other interactions.

2. Read a good book on problem solving and learn to employ the method of problem solving that is outlined in the book.

Overall, John and Mary both have similar ideals and with proper attention and support can address their respective concerns. "Although this marriage is presently in trouble, it could be a fulfilling marriage for both John and Mary. They love each other and they have common values. The problems in this relationship reside in the communication and the behavioural patterns that have evolved over a period of time. These are certainly changeable if John and Mary are *willing to work hard,* and set aside their self-interests in order to work out a satisfying and long-term relationship, which will in turn be fulfilling. Their chances of success depends entirely on *how hard they are willing to work,* and on whether they are willing to take risks and be vulnerable." (Worthington, 1998)

John and Mary have a mighty God on their side, and it is His will for the marriage to be successful. I am convinced that their relationship can be healed by God's grace, through persistent prayer and hard work.

The following is a list of components for a good marriage:

1. Mutual respect - "Husband should love his wife as he loves himself, and the wife should respect her husband." *(Eph. 5:33)*

2. Genuine commitment - The marriage vow says, "Forsaking all others." The Bible says, "For this reason a man shall leave his father and mother and be joined to his wife, and the two shall become one flesh." *(Matt. 19:5)*

3. Good communication - For genuine communication, there must be an understanding of the emotional, mental, and physical differences between men and women. There must be good communication before there could be companionship. Only then would I rather be with my spouse.

4. Time and effort - Love must be given the opportunity to mature. The climate for this is set in God's Word. When the going gets rough, a couple does not just "fall out of love;" they stay together and work things out. They do not consider themselves as martyrs of a "bad bargain," but "heirs together of the grace of life." *(1 Pet. 3:7)*

Problems and differences are resolved through forgiveness. "Be kind and compassionate to one another, forgiving each other, just as in Christ God forgave you." *(Eph. 4:32)* These words will help to safeguard your marriage and your spiritual life: "I was wrong," "forgive me," "I am sorry," and "I love you." Couples need to learn to clean up issues as soon as they develop and to erase the slate every day. "In your anger, do not sin...Do not let the sun go down while you are still angry, and do not give the devil a foothold." *(Eph. 4:26)*

5. Spiritual unity - A well-balanced marriage is a uniting of three persons – God, a man, and a woman. This is what makes marriage holy. Understanding the spiritual dimension in marriage has profound implications. Paul compared marriage – the union of husband and wife – to the eternal relationship between Christ and the church *(Eph. 5:22-33)*. Faith in Christ is the most important of all principles in the building of a happy marriage and a happy home.

Author Gary Chapman maintains, "A counsellor can never predict with absolute certainty an individual's behaviour. Based on research and personality studies, a counsellor can only predict how a person is likely to respond in a given situation." (2004) With this in mind, it is important that couples remember while there may be strong differences of opinions and personalities, counsellors (at best) may offer likely predictions for example, should couples maintain a positive approach to the mentioned suggestions, marital improvements will be made and holistic gratification experienced.

Chapter Seven

SETTING AND RESPECTING BOUNDARIES
(Is This Yours, Mine, or Ours?)

A marriage mirrors the relationship that Christ has with his bride, the church. Christ has some things that only He can do, the church has some things that only it can do, and they have some things they do together. Only Christ died and rose again. Only the church can represent Him on earth in His absence and obey his commands. Together, they work on many things, such as saving the lost. Similarly, in marriage, some duties one spouse does, some the other does, and some they do together. When the two become one on their wedding day, spouses do not lose their individual identities. Each participates in the relationship, and each has his or her own life. Marriages have two ingredients, togetherness and separateness. In a good marriage, partners carry equal loads of both. They both do things on their own, yet being apart creates a mutual longing for the other.

The problem arises when one spouse trespasses on the other's personhood. When one crosses the line and tries to control the feelings, attitudes, behaviours, choices, and values of the other, there is controversy. These things should only be controlled by each individual. When one uses control he or she crosses boundaries, and ultimately the marriage will fail. Our relationship with Christ, and any other successful relationship are based on freedom and respect.

Spouses have wants or needs of their own, and a spouse must negotiate a fair and loving relationship, and respect each other's limits. If a spouse does not set boundaries, he or she can quickly become resentful. A nagging spouse will keep the problem (power of control) going. Accepting people as they are and respecting their choices to be the way they are is executing respect. This prevents one from having the power of control over the other.

On the following table created by Cloud & Townsend (1992), there are three examples of contrast ways of reacting when taking power over what you do have power over (yourself) and giving up trying to control what you do not have power over (someone else).

Before Boundaries	After Boundaries
"Stop yelling at me. You must be nicer."	"You can continue to yell if you choose to. But I will choose not to be in your presence when you act that way."
"You have just got to stop drinking. It is ruining our family. Please listen. You are wrecking our lives."	"You may choose to not deal with your drinking if you want. But I will not continue to expose myself and the children to this chaos. The next time you are drunk, we will go to the Browns' for the night, and we will tell them why we are there. Your drinking is your choice. What I will accept is my choice."

"You are a pervert to look at pornography. That is so degrading. What kind of sick person are you anyway?"	"I will choose not to share sexually with naked women in books, magazines and television. It is up to you. I will only sleep with someone who is interested in me. Make up your mind and choose."

When you set boundaries, you should do it lovingly, and be responsible to the person in pain. Spouses who are wise and loving will accept boundaries and act responsibly toward them. Spouses who are controlling and self-centered will react angrily. Each spouse needs to respect the other's physical boundaries. Physical boundary violations can range from hurtful displays of affection to physical abuse." (Cloud & Townsend, 1992) Hurtful displays of affection include: the disregard of emotional or physical pain while continuing to inflict emotional or physical suffering. In this, one party ignores and demonstrates a lack of concern for the other party. Derogatory comments or hitting/ shoving (even as a game while the other party is pained by the behaviour) are examples of hurtful displays of affection.

The Bible says that the husband and wife have "authority" over each other's bodies. *(1 Cor. 7:4-6)* One should always remember Jesus' principle. Jesus said, "Do to others what you would have them do to you." *(Matt. 7:12)* "Husbands love your wives as your own bodies. He who loves his wife loves himself. No one ever hated his own body, but he feeds and cares for it, just as Christ does the church." *(Eph. 5:28-29)*

Given these biblical statements, the idea of slave-like submission is impossible to hold. Christ never takes away our will or asks us to do something hurtful, never pushes us past our limits, and never uses us as objects. Christ gave himself up for us and he takes care of us as he would his own body.

Balance is something that God has wired into every system. Many dimensions of a marriage need balancing: power, strength, togetherness, sex, and so on. Boundaries help create mutual balance, instead of split balance, and help couples keep each other accountable.

The goal of boundaries is to allow spouses to exercise tough love. This is the true self-denial of the New Testament. When you are in control of yourself, you can give and sacrifice for loved ones in a helpful way instead of giving into destructive behaviour and self-centeredness. This allows one to give in a way that leads to good fruits and to live up to the law of Christ that is to serve one another. Serving one another must be done out of freedom and not boundary-less compliance or control. Setting and receiving firm boundaries with your spouse can lead to greater intimacy. "Owe no man nothing but love." *(Rom. 13:8)* You show your love by loving those who God created, especially your spouse.

Being patient can motivate you to change, making you more compatible with your spouse as you modify your own behaviour that can be annoying. You will need to forbear the things about your spouse that are unchanging. In your goal to become more like Christ, you must remember that it will take a measure of forbearance and patience to motivate you to change. Forbearance does help when your goal is to be more patient. Forbearance means that there are some things in life that will not change in your lifetime. A good sense of humor is important when you are practicing forbearance.

"The laws of boundaries are about marriage as it really is. When you do loving, responsible things, people draw close to you. When you are unloving or irresponsible, people withdraw from you. You need to avoid taking ownership for your mate's life. Spouses often try to use boundaries to assert power over the other mate, and it does not work. You can influence your spouse but you do not have the power to change them. Mature adults desire the freedom of others as well as their own. Pain can be the best friend your relationship has ever had when experienced during your growth and maturity in marriage. Proactive, mature, and responsible people solve problems with patience without blowing up. The most powerful obstacle to setting boundaries in marriage is envy. Envy is miserable because you are dissatisfied with your state, yet powerless to change it. Active spouses have an edge in boundary setting. When spouses do nothing, or act passive it stifles boundary development and growth in their marriages.

Couples should not wait for their mate to take the first step, but should assume the first move in setting boundaries. Spouses must then communicate their boundaries in order for them to be successful in their marriage. *A boundary that is not communicated is a boundary that does not exist.* I believe that if all spouses practice the ten laws of boundaries by Dr. Cloud & Dr. Townsend they would definitely achieve the essentials of an hounourable marriage.

Listed below are ten laws of boundaries for marriages presented by Dr. Cloud and Dr. Townsend (1999):

1. The Law of Sowing and Reaping: Our actions have consequences.

2. The Law of Responsibility: We are responsible to each other, but not for each other.

3. The Law of Power: We have power over some things; we do not have power over others, including to change people.

4. The Law of Respect: If we wish for others to respect our boundaries, we need to respect theirs.

5. The Law of Motivation: We must be free to say no before we can wholeheartedly say yes.

6. The Law of Evaluation: We need to evaluate the pain our boundaries cause others.

7. The Law of Pro-activity: We take action to solve problems based on our values, wants, and needs.

8. The Law of Envy: We will never get what we want if we focus outside our boundaries and on what others have.

9. The Law of Activity: We need to take the initiative in setting limits rather than be passive.

10. The Law of Exposure: We need to communicate our boundaries to each other

When spouses apply these laws to their marriages, they will experience a change in relating to each other. Remember, one cannot break laws forever without consequences. Spouses have to either live in accord with them and succeed, or continually defy them and pay the consequences. These laws will help your marriage adapt to God's principles for relationship.

Chapter Eight

FORGIVENESS

One does not often recognize that the spirit of unforgiveness is within them, therefore they think that they are forgiving. However, one must ask God to reveal this to them so that they can become free from the paralyzing grip unforgiveness has on their lives.

Forgiveness must start at home because unforgiveness toward one family member will bring great devastation to the family. It is very easy to have unforgiveness toward family members because they are with you the most, know you the best, and can hurt you the deepest. Unforgiveness becomes very visible in your behaviour and cause other people to notice because unforgiveness shows in the face, words, and actions that causes people to feel uncomfortable around you. Whenever you cannot see clearly, you stumble around in confusion, make mistakes, and become weak, sick, and bitter. When you choose to forgive, you benefit, and other people are happy being around you.

The Bible clearly states the importance of forgiving your parents. The Scripture says, "Honour thy father and thy mother: that thy days may be long upon the land which the Lord thy God giveth thee." *(Ex. 20:12)* If you do not honour your parents, then your life will be shortened. You are responsible if you hold on to bitterness and unforgiveness. It is a choice to let go. It is your responsibility to confess your unforgiveness to God and ask Him to help you forgive others so that you can move on with your life in love. Ask God to reveal any unforgiveness you have toward a family member, because you are going to be miserable until you get it resolved. As a Christian, Christ has commanded you to forgive. "And forgive us our debts, as we forgive our debtors…For if ye forgive men their trespasses, your heavenly Father will also forgive you: But if you forgive not men their trespasses, neither will your Father forgive your trespasses. " *(Matt. 6:12-15)*

The power to forgive and the command to forgive have been given to you by God. Jesus said, "Therefore if you are offering your gift at the altar and there remember your brother has something against you, leave your gift there in front of the altar. First go and be reconciled to your brother; then come and offer your gift." *(Mat. 5:23-25)*

All you need to be more forgiving is a gentle reminder by the Holy Spirit of how much Christ has forgiven you. Forgiveness can flow from you to your spouse by your choice, whether your spouse is present or not. This can be a great force in your life and in your marriage since forgiveness is the gift you give – just as Christ has given it to you.

"As Christians, you are sinners saved by the grace of God. The only requirement you had to meet was a willingness to confess your sins and believe on the Lord Jesus Christ then ask God to take over your lives. Even in a good marriage with two mature Christians, there are going to be times when both marriage partners sin in their actions toward the other spouse." *(Weiss, 2005)*

Hate is a very strong word, and sometimes one may feel very strongly that they might actually have hate for another person. Forgiveness however, is to be freed from the root of hate because when unforgiving thoughts are entertained, they turn to hate from within. Jesus felt so strongly about hate that He said, "Anyone who hates his brother is a murderer, and you know that no murderer has eternal life in him." *(1 John 3:15)* He also said, "And when you stand praying, if you hold anything against anyone, forgive him, so that your Father in heaven may forgive you your sins." *(Mk. 11:25)*

Forgiveness may seem impossible because of the devastating and horrendous pain you may have suffered. If you have a hard time forgiving someone, ask God to give you a heart of forgiveness for him and pray for him. It is amazing how God softens your heart when you pray for people and your anger, resentment, and hurt turn into love.

Peter asked Jesus how many times should he forgive? Jesus said to him, "I say not unto thee, until seven times: but until seventy times seven." *(Matt.18: 21-22)* You may be able to think of someone you have to forgive seventy times seven, but God wants you to forgive as many times as it takes because He wants you to be a forgiving person.

Everything you do in life that has eternal value depends on loving God and loving others. It is much easier to love God than it is to love others, but God sees them as being the same. One of the most loving things you can do is forgive. It is hard to forgive those who have hurt, offended, or mistreated you but God wants you to love even your enemies. In the process of doing so, He perfects us, "Be ye therefore perfect, even as your Father which is in heaven is perfect." *(Matt. 5:48)*

You must ask God to help you to forgive yourself for the times you have failed and if you have blamed God for things that have happened in your life, ask Him to show you so that you can confess it before Him. This will enable you to love your enemies as He has commanded in His Word. Ask the Lord to teach you how to bless those who curse you and persecute you. The Scripture said, "But I say unto you, love your enemies, bless them that curse you, do good to them that hate you, and pray for them which despitefully use you and persecute you; that ye may be the children of your Father which is in heaven; for he maketh his sun to rise on the evil and on the good, and sendeth rain on the just and the unjust." *(Matt. 5:44-45)*

Forgiveness is possible whether the person is present or not, it will be just as complete in your heart since forgiveness is a decision. Remember that Christ died for us while we were yet sinners. Paul said, "But God commendeth his love toward us, in that, while we were yet sinners, Christ died for us." *(Rom. 5:8)* Christ did not wait for humanity to ask for forgiveness before He sacrificed himself for the forgiveness of our sins. He exercised His right and power to forgive you even though you were not present or able to ask for forgiveness two thousand years ago. Therefore, you must also exercise your right and power to forgive your spouse without your spouse repenting. It means that you can free yourself from the impact of that wrong by offering forgiveness at will.

First Corinthians Chapter 13 can help you to get a practical handle on sin. Paul said, "Love is patient, love is kind, it does not envy, does not boast, and it is not proud. It is not rude; not self-seeking; not easily angered; and it keeps no record of wrongs. Love does not delight in evil but rejoices with the truth. It always protects, always trusts, always hopes, and always perseveres. Love never fails." *(1 Cor. 13:4-8)* It is very important that you learn to be very honest about your sin and be honest with your spouse.

Chapter Nine
SERVICE

In marriage, spouses should anticipate his or her partner's spiritual, emotional, physical, and material needs and should do everything he or she can to meet them. On the night of Jesus' betrayal, Jesus took a towel and a basin of water and washed the feet of His disciples. The story is a great illustration of the call each spouse has received to serve one another. See John 13:1-17.

"Life includes grief and tribulation. Through it all, the lows and the highs, the pains and the pleasures, the sorrows and the joys, Mary loved God and looked to Him for strength that is always made perfect in weakness. Spouses should hide and treasure God's Word in their hearts; obey God's Word; submit to God's good and acceptable and perfect will for their lives; follow those whom God has appointed to lead them; nurture a heart of faith and trust God's plan and His timing. (George, 2003)

Serving is a Christian Virtue

There are many who strive to lead, but Christ calls us to serve. At one point, Jesus' disciples were arguing about which of them would be considered to be the greatest. When Jesus heard their dispute, he said to them, "The kings of the Gentiles lord over them; and those who exercise authority over them call themselves Benefactors. But you are not to be like that. Instead, the greatest among you, should be like the youngest, and the one who rules like the one who serves. For who is greater, the one who is at the table or the one who serves? Is it not the one who is at the table? But I am among you as one who serves." *(Luke 22:25-27)*

God is looking for servants in the kingdom of God. In a Christian marriage, this is also true of what God is looking for – a servant. When you are called to marriage, you are called to servitude. You are saying "I do" to serving the other person all the days of your lives. You are both called to serve each other. There are five areas of need where you must learn to serve your spouse in marriage:

1. Spiritual Service – Your spouse needs you to serve him or her spiritually. You can serve your spouse spiritually by being spiritually strong, praying, studying the Word, and developing a circle of good Christian friends. Your spouse needs you to serve by being his or her best intercessor. Care enough about your spouse's spiritual growth to ask about the spiritual lessons he or she is learning. Discuss his or her daily Bible study, and be interested in his or her one-on-one relationship with Christ. Your spouse also needs your servant's heart spiritually as you serve your children.

2. Emotional Service – Everyone needs an emotional cheerleader, someone who encourages you and lifts your spirit when you are feeling low. To serve another person emotionally does require your presence and support. An emotional servant invites his or her spouse to discover hidden feelings so he or she can understand what is going on inside. An emotional servant does not shame his or her spouse for distinct feelings and does not bring those feelings back up later to belittle that person.

Be committed to becoming your spouse's emotional servant. Keep yourself emotionally fit so that you know and understand the feelings you are experiencing within yourself. Be vulnerable yourself so your spouse will feel safe sharing his or her feelings with you. Above all, protect your spouse's heart.

3. Material Service – Material things are definitely needed for one's life to function smoothly. For example: clothing, furniture, car, etc. Couples should plan carefully, especially if they are low on funds, and only address the basic needs, bearing in mind that God told us to give back one-tenth of His blessings to Him.

4. Sexual Service – Sex is one of the greatest gifts God gives to a married couple. Sex is great and is also a place where your spouse needs your service. In this area, your spouse is totally dependent upon your Christlikeness. If one person in a marriage relationship is sexually self-centered, it will cause pain for the other spouse and will bring harm to the marriage relationship.

Serve your spouse sexually by guarding your sexuality, including forms of entertainment, conversations, etc., with others. Your sex organ belongs to God and to your spouse, not to you alone. Paul said, "Now for the matters you wrote about: It is good for a man not to marry. But since there is so much immorality, each man should have his own wife, and each woman her own husband. The husband should fulfill his marital duty to his wife, and likewise the wife to her husband. The wife's body does not belong to her alone but also to her husband. In the same way, the husband's body does not belong to him alone but also to his wife. Do not deprive each other except by mutual consent and for a time, so that you may devote yourselves to prayer. Then come together again so that Satan will not tempt you because of your lack of self-control." *(1 Cor. 7:1-5)*

You should not be entertaining lustful thoughts about others. Take the first step to healing yourself sexually so that you can serve your spouse. Sexual abuse also is an issue that impacts some marriages. You can serve your spouse by honouring his or her sexual personality and by not trying to mold him or her into your own image.

Serve your spouse sexually by saving some physical energy for him or her and make sure the bedroom door is locked so you will not be interrupted. Avoid overworking or over-cleaning, because both can wear you out; pace yourself. If you have medical or emotional issues regarding your sexuality, be prompt in attempting to resolve these issues. Everyone needs fun and entertainment in his or her life. Please do your best to serve your spouse in the area of fun.

Serve your spouse by acknowledging how your spouse relaxes. See that each one gets a fair share on your dates and vacations. If you are always doing what you want to do selfishly, you are not serving your spouse. Work together to serve each other, by including various forms of entertainment that are satisfying and fulfilling to both of you.

5. Household Service – Serve your spouse by occasionally taking on a chore that your spouse normally does – and do it well. Just as there is neither male nor female in Christ, there are no chores that are masculine or feminine. Paul said, "There is neither Jew nor Greek, there is neither bond nor free, there

is neither male nor female: for ye are all one in Christ Jesus." *(Gal. 3:28)* It is easy to find ways to serve your spouse in the home, because there are always helpful things for both of you to do around the house.

Begin your service to your spouse by making absolutely sure that you are doing at least the agreed-upon portion of what needs to be done. Not doing what you have agreed to do will create legitimate resentment in your marriage. As a Christian servant you do not want to have a "getting even" or "I did this, and you did that" mentality. Out-serve your spouse regularly – doing more than he or she does.

You must not consider yourself too good to serve your wife or your husband. She is a queen of God's and you are a king of God's, and your family is royalty. Serving each other is a spouse's duty and should be your delight. By doing so, you are showing love to each other. However, when serving each other around the house, it should be fun and it should be easy for a servant of the living God. A servant's heart makes you feel good by doing helpful things for the people you love.

Chapter Ten

RESPECT

Respecting your spouse is one of the essentials of an honourable marriage. To respect is to give honour or preference toward another. When a spouse does this, the action of respecting one another causes each spouse to become a respecter - one who demonstrates qualities of respect. Listed below are some of the examples of a respecter:

1. You are equal - A respecter comes into marriage with an idea that his or her spouse is totally equal in value. His or her spouse can reason and have a different perspective, but there is still equality between them.

2. Hearts are valuable - The respecter wants to know the mind of his or her spouse, and how he or she feels. The respecter is focused on connecting heart-to-heart. Staying in a connected relationship is more valuable to the respecter than closing the deal. The respecter values the person over outcomes.

3. Truth is a journey - The respecter knows and believes in his or her heart that he or she does not know all truth at all times. He knows that God distributes truth. There is humility in the heart of a respecter to seek truth and not presume he or she knows truth at all times.

4. No emotion justifies rudeness - A respecter is not perfect. He or she has emotions as well; therefore, he or she can dislike others, become hurt, or get angry. It is not right to be rude or unkind. Finally, the respecter knows how to have manners and how to be nice.

5. Spouses are allowed to be different - Seeing things differently, and even having different outcomes is normal for the respecter. To expect two people to agree on everything or think that one is always right is absolutely insane thinking for the respecter. It just does not make sense to believe in sameness when God intentionally and expertly made us entirely different from one another. For the respecter, it is totally acceptable to disagree – even respecters will have moments of disagreements through-out their entire lives. Navigating differences respectfully is essential to a successful marriage and with sincerity, choosing to agree to disagree is refreshing. Amos said, "Can two walk together except they be agreed." *(Amos 3.3)*

Christians should know that at a core level, it is best to treat your spouse regularly with respect and to honour your spouse with your words and with your actions. You should also know that it takes some effort not to demean, ridicule, or embarrass your spouse. Respecting another person as God respects you is encouraging that person to operate in his or her strengths. Show respect for your spouse by encouraging him or her to focus on the gifts that God has given to him or her. Show your appreciation for those gifts.

Spouses can see their partners' weaknesses, but respect comes alongside those weaknesses in a supportive manner that encourages his or her spouse to mature. Just as a spouse respects his or her children and helps them to mature out of their weaknesses, they should also respect their spouse in his or her weaknesses. In God's sight, we are all children, growing unto perfection and we are created differently. Spouses are encouraged to respect each other's differences. Respect allows the independent and different developments of each spouse's interests and gifts. A spouse who is disrespectful wants to control and stifle his or her spouse. Give respectful space to your spouse to grow and become who he or she is in the image of Christ.

Respect and disrespect can happen in an instant. Respect must display growth by changing your current negative behaviour. Keep on practicing and giving away respect, and let it flow from God through you. This will ultimately get into your spouse's heart.

The Word of God called a husband to "Live joyfully with the wife whom he loves all the days of his vain life, which He has given him under the sun – all the days of futility. For that is his portion in this life and in his work at which he toils under the sun." *(Eccl 9:9)*

When a spouse is being disrespectful to the other spouse due to a false self-image, it is difficult to get very far with that person in counselling because he or she is not being honest about himself or herself.

Ephesians 5:33 teaches that the woman's primary need is for love and the man's primary need is for respect. The husband must love his wife as he loves himself, and the wife must respect her husband. God has ordained that wives respect their husbands as a method to win husbands to Himself. As a husband opens his spirit to God, he opens his spirit to his wife. No husband feels affection toward a wife who appears to have contempt for who he is as a human being. The key to creating fond feelings of love in a husband toward his wife is through showing him unconditional respect.

Husbands are to value wives as equals. Paul's writings clearly command men to agape-love their wives. See Eph. 5:22-33. After teaching wives to behave respectfully toward their husbands, Peter goes on to tell husbands to live in an understanding way with their wives "and show her honour as a fellow heir of the grace of life."

(1 Pet. 3:1-2; 7) When Peter uses the phrase "show her honour as a fellow heir," he is telling husbands to value and prize their wives as equals within the grace of God. Paul concurs when he writes that in Christ, "there is neither Jew nor Greek, there is neither slave nor free man, there is neither male nor female; for you are all one in Christ Jesus." *(Gal. 3:28)*

Emerson Eggerchs (2004) states, "Something in a man longs for his wife to look up to him as he fulfills this role. When she does, it motivates him, not because he is arrogant, but because of how God has constructed him. Few husbands walk around claiming, "I'm first among equals." The husband with goodwill (and good sense) knows this is not his right, but it is his responsibility. The wife possesses something within that thirsts to be valued as "first in importance." Nothing energizes her more! She is not self-centered. God placed this in her by nature.

When he honours her as first in importance and she respects him as first among equals, their marriage must work. When he expects her to look up to him yet puts her down, he deflates her. When he feels she is trying to be a bossy queen, he cannot detect her real heart. When she expects him to protect her but then accuses him of being paternalistic (too fatherly) or condescending, she deflates him. When she feels he is trying to be "more than equal" or greater, she cannot detect his real heart."

Women need to learn how to understand and use the word respect because, in truth, respect is a man's deepest value. Not only do men want to serve, but they are also willing to die in combat. There is something in many men, placed there by God, to fight and die for honour, women, children, and their friends.

Chapter Eleven
KINDNESS

Human beings can feel the lack of kindness in a relationship and can feel the deprivation of kindness. Kindness is a fruit of the Spirit and there is something special in the nutrients of this fruit that makes anyone feel special. As a Christian, kindness is within you and it wants to get out. Remember that with any act of kindness you show to your spouse, you are planting the seed of kindness inside his or her spirit. In time, the seed you planted will eventually grow and the tree will bear and reap fruits of kindness. The biblical principle of sowing and reaping is very powerful. You can be kind to your spouse, eliminating any trace of meanness from your behaviour and speech. Kindness is something your spouse needs daily because kindness is the oil in a relationship. Kindness lubricates your marriage relationship because it is intentional acts of kindness in a marriage that eases the frictions in life. It is the help, the smile, and the kind words that make the responsibilities of life more tolerable and significant. We can sow words of kindness into the heart of your spouse by responding kindly to him or her. We can express kindness by the tone we use when we speak. Couples should choose the spirit in which they speak to their partner. Remember, you will reap what you sow. Please stay focused and have a kind disposition when you are communicating with your spouse.

Spouses should speak kind words during communication by making kind comments to each other in front of their friends and children and pay attention to the little and big things their spouse does for them. Always thank your spouse when he or she is serving you in some manner. Please remember, next to God, you are the loudest and most consistent voice your spouse will hear throughout his or her life. As you choose kindness, it will show up in your spoken words and give your heart a warm feeling. As your heart and words become kind, your spouse's heart also will be impacted to become kinder.

Sometimes kindness is spoken more loudly by a touch than by any words you speak. Holding your spouse's hand gently can express volumes of kindness and a gentle caress can be felt as a kind affirmation of your spouse. Sowing this type of unselfish, gentle, soft, and soothing touch is a great resource for planting kindness into your spouse's heart. The power of kindness momentarily removes the entire world and its cares from your life, allowing you to drink in pure love from your spouse. If you plant the seed of a kind touch regularly and intentionally upon your spouse the seed of kindness will grow.

It is wonderful when a husband and a wife operate in unity with a team spirit, because marriage is a team sport. You will have the greatest success if you think and act like a team and remember that your team is about both attitude and behaviour. You should know the strengths and weaknesses of each player and capitalize on each member's strengths for the good of the team. In marriage, both people win together or lose together as a team when both express genuine kindness and a good attitude.

Chapter Twelve
CELEBRATION

Choose to plant celebration in your spouse's life. It may be that some of those great characteristics in your spouse about which you bragged before marriage may have begun to appear as weaknesses. Before marriage, you may have thought your spouse was thrifty, but now you call it cheap. Once you thought your spouse was smart, but now it comes off as a know-it-all. Couples should appreciate their spouses' gifts and attributes and celebrate them personally and publicly.

With many couples it is how they think about their spouse that has changed, and not really the changes observed in their spouse. Some couples go from a spirit of celebration to a spirit of criticism toward their spouses. One of the greatest ways to celebrate your spouse is in the presence of his or her Creator and by regularly spending time praising God the Father for the spouse He gave you. You can praise God for how blessed and different you are because your spouse is in your life. Praise God for his or her attractiveness, sexuality, personality, humour, friendship, and any other attributes you want to highlight to the Father. God loves to hear you praise Him for your spouse. Celebrate your spouse before the living God and see what happens.

Our God is a celebrator; celebration is one of His characteristics. He celebrates His creation with endless amounts of colour.

Regardless of who you are or how you grew up, God is a celebrator, and He is celebrating you and your spouse constantly. You are exhibiting your Christlikeness when you are singing the same song of celebration over your spouse that God sings.

Now it is time to celebrate your spouse in front of the enemy, the devil, and any of his demons that might want to highlight your spouse's weaknesses. They start by suggesting negative thinking about your spouse. For example, your spouse is selfish, insensitive to your needs, lazy, arrogant, wilful, rebellious etc. The enemy's objective is to utilize your relationship with your spouse to cause you to hurt, criticize, or emotionally abandon him or her. The enemy knows that your spouse is the closest person to your heart. If he can get you to buy into his lies and criticize, his work is done. The Scripture says, "And I heard a loud voice saying in heaven, Now is come salvation, and strength, and the kingdom of our God, and the power of his Christ: for the accuser of our brethren is cast down, which accused them before our God day and night. And they overcame him by the blood of the Lamb, and by the word of their testimony; and they loved not their lives unto the death. *(Rev. 12:10-11)* Do remember, the enemy hates your godly spouse and the other parent to your children, because together you are raising godly seed(s) for the future battles of the kingdom.

The best way to deal with the enemy's lies about your spouse is to celebrate him or her continually. You must be aware of the enemy's tactics. Make a list of five things you really love about your spouse. Each time the enemy starts accusing your spouse, continue your vocal celebrations until you are so grateful and more in love with your spouse than before the enemy's attack. There is great power in the celebrating of your spouse. You can utilize this power to fight for your spouse instead of against him or her, and you will truly be a winner at marriage.

Celebration in the presence of others is powerful. Your spouse is wonderful. This is why someone as smart as you married him or her. Tell your children privately and publicly in front of your spouse what you like, love, admire, and appreciate about them. Also, that you depend upon your spouse. Let your spouse and your children know that you benefit greatly because your spouse is alive and married to you.

Tell your parents, their parents, your neighbours, and friends about the goodness and value of your spouse. Do this when you are alone with these people. Let others know that you are blessed because you are married to your spouse. Sing your spouse's value proudly and loudly and stop singing the old song to devalue him or her. You are the president of your spouse's fan club let others know about the ongoing celebration of your spouse because he or she is worth the celebration.

Celebrating your spouse directly is a very important aspect of celebration. There are many different ways to celebrate your spouse. For example, celebrate with inexpensive gifts, a handwritten card or note - that is the best way to celebrate your spouse. Surprise him or her with a favourite coffee, tea, juice, soft drink, or take your spouse to a favourite restaurant for a long lunch and celebrate him or her through spoken words. Spending time with your spouse and doing something he or she really likes to do will send a clear message that you really celebrate this aspect about him or her. Stop for a moment and evaluate some ways that God has made your spouse stronger than you, just as there are some strengths that you have that your spouse does not have. You can have a celebration that can change the atmosphere and the dynamics in your marriage.

"When compassion is strong, you should find yourself naturally desiring what is best for the other person. You should not be threatened by the thought of your spouse's success and you should rejoice with him or her. The requirements of 1 Cor. 13 and Eph. 5:21-33 are guidelines that are natural to fulfill. There are times when you feel jealous or fearful of losing the other's affection because humanity invades every relationship. Overall, you should feel comfortable with your spouse developing their gifts, having successful experiences and even special friendships outside of your own. When the other suffers a disappointment, you should feel it also." (Smith, 2000)

Chapter Thirteen

DEMONSTRATING CHRISTLIKE LOVE IN MARRIAGE

When spouses are committed to the essentials of an honourable marriage, faithfulness, patience, forgiveness, service, respect, kindness, and celebration can be used as practical strategies for demonstrating Christlike love in marriage. These are the very elements that allow you opportunities for growth, development, and maturity into the image of Christ. In reality, many spouses experience disturbances, disruptions, and conflicts in their marriage, but through prayer, fasting, and counselling they can enjoy and maintain a rewarding and successful marriage.

Pain comes with life and relationships and is an intended part of the process for us to become Christlike. Reality is acknowledging the fact that you may have been hurt in the past and will likely experience pain in the present and in the future. It would be wise to acknowledge the presence of pain in your life – past, present, and future and learn how to deal with it. All human relationships have pain and healthy people accept pain as a part of life. How you deal with pain in your life makes all the difference. Whether you deal with the pain by choosing to work through it positively and thereby keeping your relationship in tact or by not addressing pain, which ultimately has its own set of negative outcomes.

In marriage, it is most likely that your spouse has disappointed you in the past, and will disappoint you in the future, and you have probably caused some disappointments for your spouse as well. Be aware that marriage is not perfect. Once you accept this, you will no longer respond to disappointment as a personal insult. This inherent conflict in marriage is part of the life process. "When couples are experiencing disappointment, they must remember that their spouse is not the enemy. Spouses must trust God and cooperate with Him to fulfill all the dreams He gives them and remember that Satan is their enemy. Couples can choose to protect themselves from his attack; to cultivate the possibilities they yet can accomplish; to use their talents, skills, and abilities for the good of others; and to live within the laws of limitation that govern who they can become. These keys to maximizing potential, together with the keys to releasing potential, acknowledges both their dependence on God and their responsibility to trust Him and cooperate with Him as He works in and through them.

Be aware of the enemies of your potential: sin, disobedience, fear, discouragement, procrastination, past failures, the opinions of others, distractions, success, tradition, a wrong environment, comparison, opposition, and society's pressure. Remember that God's power is stronger than all the enemies of your potential." (Munroe, 1992)

This is about being Christlike and seeking the truth as an opportunity to grow and not about who is right and who is wrong. Couples must understand this powerful biblical principle: "Charity never faileth: but whether there be prophecies, they shall fail; whether there be tongues, they shall cease; whether there be knowledge, it shall vanish away." *(1 Cor. 13:8)* It is wonderful that love never fails, even though we know that we can fail. Love is the cornerstone of marriage. Spouses will find themselves in an emotional battle to love when they feel hurt, misunderstood, tired, or just want to argue. The essentials of an honourable marriage are tools for taking control of their behaviour in their marriage that will result in ultimate success.

Take all your effort with prayer and focus it on one essential at a time. For example, if you are working on kindness, choose one of your goals on the kindness list and stay focused with prayer, measure your progress and be consistent in your goal of kindness until you know you have achieved all your goals. You will be able to see the measurements you logged as showing proof that you are actually much kinder today than you were weeks or months ago.

It is crucial that you measure your progress to evaluate how successful you are in your marital growth. Soon you will be amazed to see the change in the way you behave, the way you feel and think about your spouse. Choose an accountability partner of the same gender and review your goals and progress with him or her at least once per week. If your accountability partner is agreeable, pray about each other's goals to improve your marriage. The level of friendship you have with your accountability partner as you pray, laugh, and encourage each other through this season of your change will definitely help improve your marriage. Your written notes will demonstrate your strategies and the victories you have won. The tactics you used will assure your success. Due to changing your behaviour from your old tactics, your spouse is forced to face a growth opportunity. There may be times when he or she faces this new opportunity graciously, but at other times your change may create real conflict. For example, if your spouse has not been helping as he or she should, and you continue serving your spouse consistently for several months, you are sharing and experiencing Christlike love. Your spouse's aims for preventing your efforts become less of a distraction and are no longer effective. In this, your spouse now has an opportunity to grow out of resentment and anger because of your continued service.

The changes that you make probably will cause some conflict or confrontation. Conflict is inevitable and guaranteed in a marriage relationship if you are actively and intentionally changing from your former "tactics" to more effective "strategies." When conflict comes, patiently stay consistent because your consistency will bring results, and your consistency is crucial for you to ultimately succeed in your marriage. The Scripture says, "And let us not be weary in *well doing*: for in due season we shall reap, if we faint not." *(Gal. 6:10)*

Spouses cannot think of anything better than trying to love each other more than before. Remember that a harvest takes time and nurturing, therefore it will take time for your spouse to trust any new behaviour. As time and consistency occur, he or she will begin to trust this new behaviour; therefore, be patient as you go through the changes.

The essentials of an honourable marriage are pathways for new growth because you are not capable of always being loving or perfect, it is a growth process. Stay real, and avoid the "always" and "never" traps. You will need to be patient with yourself as you grow. Some days you will be very successful and other days you might feel like a failure.

Somewhere along the path of false accusations, beatings, and crucifixion, Jesus might have been tempted to say, "That is enough!" Yet He never lost sight of His long-term goal: "the joy set before Him," which was for our salvation. He continued in the battle until He won the victory. Please be encouraged and stay focused on loving your spouse, because it is worth experiencing a victorious marriage with your lifetime partner.

As soon as your motivation moves from pleasing Jesus, and trying not to be more like Him, to needing appreciation from your spouse, you can, and probably will get disappointed, hurt, and discouraged. Please make your actions something between Jesus and you alone, instead of something between you and your spouse. When you serve all day, and did not receive a smile, you can complain to Jesus and He will smile with you and tell you that He is proud of you.

God is forever faithful and loves when you serve your spouse with love, respect and honour. When you fall into self-pity or frustration, it is usually a sign you want appreciation. Do not look to your spouse to fill your cup, look to Jesus and listen to his voice. He knows how to pour praise into an honest heart that is trying to love His child, your spouse. Remember as you go forward, you are not going alone. God is with you. This is a great journey you can take by yourself and, by the grace of God, your spouse will follow your example.

Give your spouse a chance to see faithfulness, patience, forgiveness, service, respect, kindness, and celebration soaring daily in your life. Soar, and let him or her watch. If your spouse chooses to join you in the flight, that is great, but if not, you are the power of one, enticing others to the great flight of becoming more like Jesus.

Chapter Fourteen
FRUITS OF THE SPIRIT

Christians are planting something in their lives each day, and are also reaping whatever they have sown. It is important to plant and nurture the right seeds belonging to the fruit of the Spirit because you will reap the good and the bad for years after you have sown. Jesus said, "I am the vine, ye are the branches: He that abideth in me, and I in him, the same bringeth forth much fruit: for without me ye can do nothing." *(John 15:5)* When you share your life with Jesus, His likeness is stamped on your spirit and soul and when you plug into him, the fruit of his Spirit is manifested in you.

The fruit of the Spirit is love, joy, peace, patience, kindness, goodness, faithfulness, gentleness, and self-control.

1. Love – Spouses should ask God to plant His love in their hearts in a profound and powerful way so that they are able to fully experience His love, which will flow through them to others.

2. *Joy* – Spouses can have joy in spite of their circumstances that no matter how difficult and painful it seems, they will still experience the joy that comes through a close, intimate relationship with the Lord.

3. Peace – Spouses should pray that the presence of the Lord be planted in their lives. His presence provides the sort of peace that is beyond comprehension. Spouses should pray that His peace will grow strong and prevail no matter what their circumstances are.

4. Patience - It is important to God that spouses grow in patience as He perfects and refines them. Trials will come because it develops patience.

5. Kindness – Spouses must demonstrate kindness to each other. Paul said, "Put on therefore, as the elect of God, holy and beloved, bowels of mercies, kindness, humbleness of mind, meekness, longsuffering; forbearing one another, and forgiving one another, if any man has a quarrel against you: even as Christ forgave you, so also do ye." *(Col. 3:12-13)* The ultimate act of kindness was demonstrated when Jesus gave His life for us, and even continues to forgive us when we sin.

6. Goodness - When the goodness of God is sown in your spouse's soul it leads them to produce good deeds. The Scripture says, "A good man out of the good treasure of the heart bringeth forth good things." *(Matt. 12:35)*

7. Faithfulness - When spouses are solid, steadfast, dependable, reliable, loyal, and trustworthy and do what is right no matter what, they exhibit faithfulness.

8. Gentleness - Gentleness is a humble meekness that is calm, soothing, peaceful, and easy to be around. The Scripture says, "But the wisdom that is from above is first pure, then peaceable,

gentle, and easy to be entreated, full of mercy and good fruits, without partiality, and without hypocrisy." *(Jam. 3:17)*

9. Self-control - Only God can plant self-control into people's heart and cause them to bear fruit of self-control. Having no self-control means you do whatever pleases you whenever you please, no matter what the consequences. Pray that you will not be powerless against the forces that tug on your soul.

Chapter Fifteen

MEN AND WOMEN ARE EQUAL BUT DIFFERENT

Men and women were created equal but different. Everything was designed by God to fulfill His purpose. Females and males are different because of their design. Different does not mean inferior or superior. The purposes of women and men determine their individual nature and needs. The female and male were both given dominion over the earth, yet they each execute this purpose according to their unique purposes and designs.

"Adam and Eve rejected God's purposes by an act of their wills but still God's purposes cannot be altered. Because of the fall, man experienced broken fellowship with God and both spiritual, and physical death. They also experienced the loss of the perfectly balanced relationship between them and God. As a result of the fall, God did not curse the female or the male; He cursed the earth. They experienced the natural consequences of rejecting God and His purposes. The woman has a desire to please her husband and the man has a desire to dominate her also because of the fall.

The male was created to be the provider of his family. Work was given to the male to advance the purposes of God and to bring fulfillment while using the skills and abilities God gave him. Man was given work before the woman was created. God gave the man, not the woman, the responsibility for being the main provider of the family. A husband won't always be able to immediately change his financial circumstances so that his wife does not have to work. He just needs to move toward the ideal by working toward this goal. A provider anticipates needs before they arrive. He plans, prepares, and makes provision for those needs. The male was created to be the protector of his family and everything else for which he is responsible. Paul says, "Now I want you to realize that the head of every man is Christ, and the head of the woman is man, and the head of Christ is God." *(1 Cor. 11:3)* This means a man does not need to be married to be responsible for women. Through these attributes, a male is designed to protect everything he is responsible for: physical strength, logical thinking, a sense of territorial protectiveness, and the drive to excel, and his own ego. God has given men the ability, strength, and spiritual knowledge to protect and guard everything He has entrusted to their care. Without the awareness that men and women are supposed to be different, they become at odds with each other. They usually become angry or frustrated with the opposite sex because they do not know this important truth. They expect the opposite sex to be more like themselves. They desire them to "want what they want" and to "feel the way they feel." This attitude sets them up to be disappointed and prevents them from taking the necessary time to communicate lovingly about their differences." *(Munroe, 2001)*

Men mistakenly expect women to think, communicate, and react the way men do and vice versa. They have forgotten that men and women are supposed to be different because they were created differently. As a result, their relationships are filled with unnecessary friction and conflict. Clearly recognizing and respecting these differences dramatically reduce confusion when dealing with the opposite sex.

Jesus Christ, the Redeemer, saved humanity from its fallen state and restored the relationship and partnership between male and female.

Chapter Sixteen

DEALING WITH ANGER

Some people experience many challenges when dealing with anger and need help to control it. Most times, it is recommended that they attend Anger Management classes to learn self-control. Anger damages intimate relationships. "Chronic anger makes people rigid and highly defensive, and the long-term effect is a loss of empathy and intimacy. Angry partners feel helpless and think that if the other partner would only change or improve, things would feel better because it always feels like the other person's fault. While anger focuses on the other person, on how he or she does wrong and needs to change, healthy coping brings the focus back on you." *(McKay & Paleg, 1994)*.

When a wife or a husband experiences significant trauma from his or her spouse or others, they become wounded. You can learn to deal with the anger you have toward your spouse either by being prayerful or seeking help from a Christian counsellor. Couples must overcome the hurt that happens in marriage in order to experience joyful moments with each other. This pain may be from family of origin issues caused by neglect, abuse, abandonment, childhood sexual abuse, rape, etc. Some couples carry their pain in their spirit that is sometimes inflicted by their spouse. In some Christian marriages, spouses traumatize one another or deprive one another to such a degree that the anger appears overwhelming.

"Anger can build up in your soul until the size of your wounds makes it difficult to be intimate. Although you did not cause the wounds, you are now responsible to heal from them. Unfortunately, you are 100% responsible to heal from the wound, even [when] your spouse is 100% responsible for causing the wound. Some people enjoy creating pain for others. If you have wounds others have inflicted on your life, be assured that God [will] be with you in the process but you must be obedient and not allow the pain from the past to justify why you [are] not becoming all that you could be." *(Cloud & Townsend, 1992)*

Even if your spouse caused the pain, he or she cannot heal you. Your spouse can say, "I am sorry" but that does not get rid of the pain that has already been placed inside your soul. You need to get God's help and counselling to deal with the problem and receive your healing. The experience of forgiveness is a great asset for you as you move forward in experiencing the essentials of an honourable marriage.

"It takes great grace, discipline and desire to come to a place where you can consistently hear God's voice. You must meet this challenge, for it is the key that opens every door. It may be hard for you to listen because it often takes time for you to hear from God. It takes the ability to wait in His presence, to quiet your minds and your hearts so that the static and noise that often keep you deaf to His gentle voice will melt away, and you can hear Him at last. 'Wait on the LORD: be of good courage, and He shall strengthen thine heart: wait, I say, on the LORD, (Psalm 27:14).'" *(Hammond, 1995)*

Chapter Seventeen
LOVE

Agape is the supreme love of God shown in Christ when He died for the ungodly. It means meeting another person's needs even if your own needs are not being met. It is a love that reaches beyond the normal limits, even to the point of seeking the highest good of one's enemies. The highest form of love is possible only as we allow God to live through us. It is a fruit of the Spirit, a quality that can be produced only by God. Christians are called to be like God in demonstrating this love to others. The Bible calls love the greatest virtue. Paul said, "and now abideth faith, hope, love, these three; but the greatest of these is love." *(1 Cor. 13:13)*

Within churches around the world there are broken relationships – brokenness in families, brokenness between husbands, wives, mothers, fathers, sons and daughters, and between members of churches but kindness, mercy, loving-kindness, unfailing love, tenderness, and faithfulness are necessary elements and are to be maintained and experienced within communities of faith – the Christian church. "For God so loved the world that He gave His one and only Son, that whoever believes in Him shall not perish but have eternal life." *(John 3:16)* Spouses should give love. They should nourish and cherish their relationship and thereby experience happiness and life within their marriage instead of giving hate that brings destruction and causes them to experience unhappiness and divorce that is death to their marriages. Micah says, "He hath showed thee, O man, what is good; and what doth the Lord require of thee, but to do justly, and to love mercy, and to walk humbly with thy God." *(Micah. 6:8)*

Spouses should embark on a new area of openness as they practice the essentials of an honourable marriage. Christians will certainly be helped as they build their marriage on firm foundations, and broken or wounded marriage relationships can be healed. Paul said, "For God hath not given us the spirit of fear; but of power, and of love, and of a sound mind." *(2 Tim. 1:7)* Love is the primary ingredient of Christian discipline. Sometimes when everything has been exhausted, love stands with an outstretched hand though saying nothing and doing nothing, presents itself as simply available.

Many Christians enter marriages today with their own set of expectations and desires and when their spouses do not live up to them, they are disappointed, hurt, and frustrated. God designed marriage to be a permanent, meaningful, truly fulfilling, and joyful relationship. Spouses are likely to miss that fulfillment if they do not know God's plans, or if they have not asked for His counsel. Even if your mate insists on walking away, and abandoning you, you still need to understand God's precepts and alternatives for you. It is impossible for God's love to be passive because it must act. God acted in love for us by sending His Son to pay the penalty our wicked deeds deserved and gave us eternal life. In the same way, we cannot say that we love our spouses and then do nothing. We too must demonstrate our love with action. Without love, marriage lacks the motivational foundation upon which the structure should be built.

Love fulfills our basic need for self-esteem. Self-esteem, like self-image, is one of the basic components of human identity. Satisfaction of the need for self-esteem leads to feelings of worth and usefulness to others. Failure to meet that need produces feelings of inferiority and helplessness. Genuine love and tenderness is the stronger bending to the weak. Love is something that serves, that relieves actual need; it is the spirit of the good Samaritan who poured oil and wine into the wounds of the injured person and helped the fallen to their feet. The person who can love most fervently, despite the faults and imperfections of others, is definitely modeling the love of the Lord Jesus Christ. You must seek ways to bring about right relationship without allowing it to destroy your self-esteem. Men become husbands as they marry and fathers as they reproduce. Women become wives and then mothers. Children are not simply kids, but someone's children. Humans are constantly in relationship because God made them to be social and not to live in isolation. People must fellowship and interact with one another in order to be happy. All relationships must be nourished and cultivated, or they will eventually die.

The good news is that Christ came to restore relationships. God is the Healer who makes you whole, who restores their fellowship with Him, who binds spouses together and helps them see the need for unity in their marriage. Relationships are successful when taken seriously, built on integrity as they are developed and worked on. Relationships are dynamic, changing, affected by circumstances, often painful, and can be difficult. It requires sustenance to help them grow and it is important that relationships be structured, nurtured, and preserved. There should be equal value in relationships because selfishness destroys relationships. For example, couples cannot enjoy the fruits of a happy marriage without contributing to the happiness and well-being of their spouses. They cannot maintain proper relationship with their spouses without valuing their experiences and without avoiding manipulating each other. Couples relationships with God can also be affected if they do not reciprocate God's provisions of grace in love, worship, and praise. God's love, and His will, brought about all that was necessary for our salvation.

Christians are in relationship with God, and although they cannot reciprocate all that God gives, they must respond appropriately to

God's great gift. They must respond in service, obedience, worship, praise, repentance, sincerity, faith and love. The marriage relationship will certainly succeed when spouses remember to marvel at God's gift of love. They should thank God for His tough love, the love that brings about all that is required, whether it is His own sacrifice or the giving of what they need to become the person God wants them to be. They should also respond to God's love in repentance and in love.

The first and most important of all relationships is the one you enjoy with God. God recognizes the need for human companionship. The second most important relationship is the one between husband and wife. It is a fine line between true love and manipulation. True love is not manipulative or abusive and it seeks the good of its object. It is not jealous, it wants happiness for its object, and it is pleased when he or she grows into a whole and happy human being. Manipulation disguises itself as love, but is in reality selfishness (self-love).

"Psychologists have observed that among human basic needs are the need for security, self-worth, and significance. For example, if spouses feel loved by their mate, he or she can relax, knowing that his or her lover will do him or her no ill and will feel secure in their presence. They will feel that they can face many uncertainties in their vocation, have enemies in other areas of their lives, but they will feel secure with their partners." *(Chapman, 2004)*

The need for significance is the emotional force behind much of our behaviour. Life is driven by the desire for success. People want their lives to count for something and they have their own idea of what it means to be significant. They work hard to reach their goals. Feeling loved by a spouse enhances the other spouse's sense of significance. People reason that if someone loves them, they must have significance.

When spouses lovingly invest time, energy, and effort in their partners, there partners will believe that they are significant. Without love, they may spend a lifetime in search of significance, self-worth, and security. When they experience love, it impacts all of those needs positively. Spouses are now freed and able to develop their potential. They are more secure in their self-worth and can now turn their efforts outward instead of being obsessed with his or her own needs. True love always liberates.

In the context of marriage, if you do not feel loved your differences are magnified and spouses come to view each other as a threat to their happiness. They fight for self-worth and significance, and marriage becomes a battlefield rather than a haven.

"In the security of love, a couple can discuss differences without condemnation, and conflicts can be resolved. In the mystery of marriage where two becomes one, although male and female are different they can learn to live together in harmony. They will discover how to bring out the best in each other and obtain the rewards of love. Learning your spouses primary love language can make potential a reality in an honourable marriage. The emotional need is at the center of human emotional desires. The need for love from childhood follows into adulthood and also into marriage. Humans need love before they 'fall in love,' and they will need it as long as they live.

The need to feel loved by one's spouse is at the heart of marital desires. Something in our nature cries out to be loved by another. Isolation is devastating to the human psyche. That is why solitary confinement is considered the cruellest of punishments. At the heart of mankind's existence is the desire to be intimate and to be loved by another. Marriage is designed to meet that need for intimacy and love. That is why the ancient biblical writings spoke of the husband and wife becoming "one flesh." That did not mean individuals would lose their identity; it meant that they would enter each other's lives in a deep and intimate way. The New Testament writers challenged both the husband and the wife to love each other." *(Chapman, 2004)*

Each spouse comes to marriage with a different personality and history, and they bring emotional baggage into their marriage relationship. They come with different expectations, different ways of approaching things, and different opinions about what matters in life. In a healthy marriage, that variety of perspectives must be processed. They need not agree on everything, but they must find a way to handle their differences so that they do not become frustrated. Couples tend to argue and withdraw, and some may tend to be violent verbally or physically in their arguments without love. When love is present, they create a climate of friendliness, a climate that seeks to understand, that is willing to allow differences and to negotiate problems. Meeting the emotional need for love affects the marriage tremendously.

The ability to love, especially when your spouse is not loving you, may seem impossible. Such love may require us to draw upon our spiritual resources because God provides the inner spiritual energy to love, even when love is not reciprocated. Remember, as Jesus died, He prayed for those who crucified Him saying, "Father, forgive them for they know not what they do." *(Lk. 23:34)* That is love's ultimate expression.

Dr. Benjamin Carson (1992) said, "If people think big, they will transform their relationships and their world. I suggest that spouses practice the following list, 'Think Big,' because I believe that it will help them as they grow and succeed in their marriages.

When you love yourselves, then you can love others. You must have a healthy regard for your own person and well being before you can really care for someone else. Loving yourself, means that you are able to make healthy choices for yourself. You will do what is right and not what would place your well being in danger. It is natural and normal to seek to survive, because God placed the survival instinct in humans. It is good to love yourselves for then you value yourselves, seek your good, and value the relationships between yourselves and others. When these relationships are valued, then they are nourished and developed. When you value yourselves and your vision of what is good, then you will seek to maximize the good you see so that others may partake of it"

The following is an example of Dr. Carson's 'Think Big' List:

T = TALENT

If you recognize your talents, use them appropriately, and choose a field that uses those talents, you will rise to the top of your field.

H = HONESTY

If you live by the rule of honesty and accept your problems, you can go far down the road of achievement.

I = INSIGHT

If you observe, reflect and commit yourselves to giving your best, you will come out on top.

N = NICE

If you are nice to others, others respond to you in the same way – and you can give your best for each other.

K = KNOWLEDGE

If you make every attempt to increase your knowledge in order to use for human good, it will make a difference in you and in your world.

B = BOOKS

If you commit yourselves to reading, thus increasing your knowledge, only God limits how far you can go in this world.

I = IN-DEPTH KNOWLEDGE

If you develop in-depth knowledge, it will enable you to give your best to others and help to make a better world.

G = GOD

If you acknowledge your need for God, He will help you.

People who love God with all their hearts, minds, and souls and who love their neighbours as themselves, demonstrates true selflessness. When Jesus said that you are to be neighbours to people outside your communities and families, he was saying that you are to love the people who cannot return your love, who do not support you, who do not reciprocate your acts of kindness, who may never be able to repay you or even express gratitude for your help. You are to love because it is your nature to love, not because you will be benefited by your actions.

"If God is love, then His people should be loving. If God nurtures relationships, then His people should nurture relationships. If God seeks the good of the objects of His love, then His people should seek the good of those they love, including God, family, friends, neighbours, enemies, and themselves. Remember, do not short-change life by failing to love, for of all things in life, love never fails." (White, 1998)

The following are four types of people in marriage relationships:

1. "There are people in *regular situations* who, married and wanting to grow, find themselves, like Adam and Eve, pointing the finger at their spouse and getting stuck. But, by removing the 'log' from their eyes, they take responsibility for their own actions, and their self-control leads to deeper love. They discover that growth is an ongoing journey, and they travel the road willingly.

2. There are people in *difficult situations* who, because of some odd teaching or their own weaknesses, have not taken the stand they need to take against hurt or evil in their marriages. They have been too afraid to stand up to the abuser, controller, or other destructive behaviour that destroys love. As a result, the behaviour and their hurt have continued. Some people choose what is good after learning that God stands up for good and against evil. God stands up for responsibility and freedom and against domination and control. They set boundaries against evil and protect good things, like love and respect. As one spouse takes a courageous stance, their marriage is turned around and saved.

3. There are people *who have done the right thing,* who have taken a stand for good, and who have been rejected. To an abusive or addicted spouse, they may have stood up and said, "This is not right." They have suffered for their stand, and the outcome was partially good: the abuse or the infliction of pain stopped, but the abusive spouse did not change, but turned against the victim. The victim found love and support from their families, friends, and their communities.

4. There are people who are *self-serving* and use boundaries to continue in denial and blame. They do not remove the log from

their own eye and seek to control themselves; instead, they blame others and try to judge and control them. Look to yourselves first, before blaming others, and make sure that you do not fall into this group. Then, take a stand for what is right and good, at all times, while guarding against using your freedom as an opportunity for selfishness.

All spouses should remember that God took control of Himself and took a stand for the good things of life, like love, forgiveness, freedom, and responsibility. He is full of mercy, and He desires for others to move out of darkness and join Him in the marvellous light. God did not achieve love at the expense of others, but only at his own expense. With God as your model, full of grace and truth, we are confident that having good boundaries in marriage is truly attainable." *(Cloud & Townsend, 1999)*

God is a God of wholeness, not of brokenness. Marital couples should be whole and complete in their marriages. Although marriage is a peculiar union, it could be a very difficult relationship. As with all relationships, one should try to put more in than the other person puts in. If one of the spouses see the good of the other and both are unselfish then the relationship will thrive. I believe that if spouses follow God's example as Dr. Cloud & Dr. Townsend suggested, they both will get more out of their marriages than they ever dreamed possible.

The love that caused Christ to die is the same love that sends the Holy Spirit to live in you and guide you every day. The power that raised Christ from the dead is the same power that saved you and is available to you in your daily life. After Jesus lifts you into God's presence, you are free to obey – out of love, and not out of necessity, and through God's power, not your own. Remember that if you stumble, you will be caught and held in Christ's loving arms.

Therefore, love and be loved. True love fulfills and does not destroy; it reflects God and does not reflect sin; true love is self-giving and the other-receiving. It is God's plan for humankind. From the beginning, LOVE is GOD'S gift to the creatures on whom He has lavished so much love and it motivates them to work hard to keep the relationship alive, healthy, and growing.

Marriage is not the end of an achievement, but the beginning of a glorious exploration and adventure into a life of infinite riches, including love, grace, truth, beauty, ecstatic pleasure, and supreme life. By applying the noted essentials of an honourable marriage, success within the marriage union is inevitable.

The goal of this book is to encourage shared growth between spouses and to increase understanding along with useful recommendations. It is my hope that having read this book, married couples will recognize God's love for them and they will achieve the joys of a rewarding marriage.

Bibliography

The Amplified Topical Reference Bible. Grand Rapids, Michigan: Zondervan Publishing House, 2006.

Arthur, Kay. A Marriage Without Regrets. Eugene, Oregon: Harvest House Publishers, 2000.

Carson, Benjamin, and Lewis Gregg. Take the Risk: Learning to Identify, Choose, and Live with Acceptable Risk. Grand Rapids, Michigan: Zondervan Publishing House, 2008.

Carson, Benjamin, with Cecil Murphey. Think Big: Unleashing Your Potential for Excellence. Grand Rapids, Michigan: Zondervan Publishing House, 1992.

Chapman, Gary. The Five Love Languages: How to Express Heartfelt Commitment to Your Mate. Chicago, U.S.A. Northfield Publishing, 2004.

Clinton, Tim & Sibcy, Gary. Attachments: Why You Love, Feel and Act the Way You Do. Brentwood, TN: Integrity Publishers, 2002.

Cloud, Henry & Dr. Townsend, John. Boundaries: When to Say Yes, When to Say No, To Take Control of Your Life. Grand Rapids, Michigan: Zondervan Publishing House, 1992.

Cloud, Henry & Townsend, John. Boundaries in Marriage: Understanding the Choices That Make or Break Loving Relationships. Grand Rapids, Michigan: Zondervan Publishing House, 1999.

Covey, Stephen R. The 7 Habits of Highly Effective People: Powerful Lessons in Personal Change. New York, NY: Simon & Schuster, Inc., 1989.

Eggerchs, Emerson. Love & Respect: The Love She Most Desires. The Respect He Desperately Needs. Nashville, Tenneessee: Thomas Nelson Inc., 2004.

Garland, Diana s. Richmond, Garland, David, E. Beyond Companionship Christians in Marriage. Eugine, Oregon: Wipf and Stock Publishers, 2003.

George, Elizabeth. The Remarkable Women of the Bible. Eugene, Oregon: Harvest House Publishers, 2003.

Graham, Billy. The Christian Worker's Handbook: A Topical Guide with Biblical Answers to the Urgent Concerns of Our Day. Charlotte, NC: World Wide Publications, 2001.

Gray, John, Ph. D. Men are From Mars; Women are From Venus. New York, NY: Harper Collins Publishers Inc., 1992.

Hammond, Lynne. The Master is Calling: Discovering the Wonders of Spirit-Led Prayer. New Kensington, PA: Whitaker House, 1995.

Holy Bible. King James Version. USA: Thomas Nelson, Inc., 1990.

Kirwan, William T. Biblical Concepts for Christian Counselling: A Case for Integrating Psychology and Theology. Grand Rapids, MI: Baker Publishing Group, 1984.

Lerner, Ph.D., Harriet. The Dance of Anger: A Woman's Guide to Changing the Patterns of Intimate Relationships. New York, NY: Harper & Row, Publishers, Inc., 1989.

Life Application Study Bible NIV. Wheaton, IL: Tyndale House Publishers, Inc. and Zondervan Publishing House. 1991.

McKay, Matthew, Ph.D.; Fanning, Patrick; and Paleg, Kim, Ph.D. Couple Skills: Making Your Relationship Work. Oakland, CA: New Harbinger Publications, Inc. 1994.

Morris, Gilbert. The Virtuous Woman. Bloomington, Minnesota: Bethany House Publishers, 2005.

Munroe, Myles. Maximizing Your Potential: The Keys to Dying Empty. Shippensburg, PA: Destiny Image Publishers, Inc., 2003.

Munroe, Myles. Understanding Your Potential: Discovering the Hidden You. Shippensburg, PA: Destiny Image Publishers, Inc., 2002.

Munroe, Myles. Understanding the Purpose and Power of Woman: A Book for Women and the Men Who Love Them. New Kensington, PA: Whitaker House, 2001.

Munroe, Myles. Understanding the Purpose and Power of Men: A Book for Men and the Women Who Love Them. New Kensington, PA: Whitaker House, 2001.

Omartian, Stormie. Lord I want to be Whole: The Power of Prayer and Scripture in Emotional Healing. Nashville: Tennessee. Thomas Nelson, Inc., 2000.

Omartian, Stormie. The Power of a Praying Wife. Eugene, Oregon: Harvest House Publishers, 1997.

Omartian, Stormie . The Power of a Praying Woman. Eugene, Oregon: Harvest House Publishers, 2002.

Peal, Norman Vincent. The Power of Positive Thinking. New York, NY: Prentice Hall Press, 1987.

Rainey, Dennis and Barbara. Moments Together for Couples: Devotions for Drawing Near to God and One Another. Ventura, CA: Regal Books, 1995.

Sandford, John & Paula. Healing the Wounded Spirit. Tulsa, OK: Victory House, Inc., 1985.

Schaefer, M. T. & Olson, D. H. (1981) Assessing intimacy: The PAIR Inventory, Journal of Marital and Family Therapy, 1, 47-60.

Schlessinger, Laura. The Proper Care & Feeding of Marriage. New York, NY: Harper Collins Publishers, Inc., 2007.

Smith, Blain M. Should I Get Married.: Downers Grove, IL: InterVarsity Press. 2000.

Walker, Paul. How to Keep Your Joy. Nashville, Tennessee: Thomas Nelson, Inc., 1987.

Weiss, Douglas. Intimacy: A 100-Day Guide to Lasting Relationships. Lake Mary, FL: Siloam Press, 2003.

Weiss, Douglas PHD. The Seven (7) Love Agreements: Decisions You Can Make on Your Own to Strengthen Your Marriage. Lake Mary, FL: Siloam Press, 2005.

White, Robert with White, Vardaman. Circle of Love: Happiness in Loving Relationships. U.S.A: Spirit Life Books, 1998

Worthington, Jr. Everett L. Marriage Counselling: A Christian Approach to Counselling Couples. Downers Grove, IL: InterVarsity Press, 1989.

CPSIA information can be obtained at www.ICGtesting.com
Printed in the USA
LVOW06s1705220315

431529LV00001B/1/P